For Mom / B.J.

on your 60th birthday!
Happy Birthday!
With love,
    Kate, Dave,

Can't wait to copy some of
FRANK's innovative ideas. Thanks for
turning me on to his architechture.
Love you mom - Kevin

all the love you need.
    FROM me

        Love
        Alexander

FRANK LLOYD WRIGHT
INSIDE AND OUT

DIANE MADDEX

BARNES & NOBLE

NEW YORK

CONTENTS

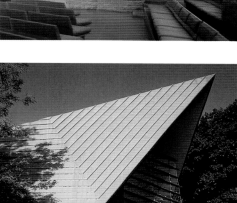

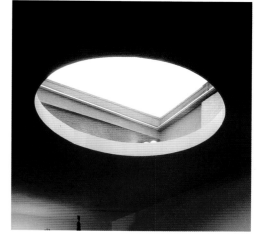

INTRODUCTION

At the beginning of the twentieth century, when other architects were designing buildings from the outside in, Frank Lloyd Wright began to work from the inside out. For him the space enclosed within the walls was "the *reality*" of a building and thus should determine its outward appearance. As he later discovered, this "new idea in architecture" was actually old—the Chinese philosopher Lao Tzu had expressed a similar concept two millennia earlier. But Wright's revelation, as he was designing the groundbreaking Unity Temple in Oak Park, Illinois, in 1905, helped him change the course of modern architecture. He left behind the conception of style as something pasted onto a box and pursued the alternative that form and function are one.

As fussy Victorian styles were being replaced by the revival of classical ideals from ancient Greece and Rome, Wright rejected such passing architectural fads—calling them "tombs of a life that has been lived." He opted instead to adhere to a set of principles that governed his work over a seven-decade career. American democracy provided a metaphor for an architecture that was equally freedom-loving. In nature he found not just forms, textures, and colors but also the basic idea that a building should grow organically from the land as a tree rises from the soil. Intrinsic to this principle of organic architecture was the vision that inside and outside should be organically unified rather than separate spheres. Wright set out to let "the room inside be the architecture outside" and left a legacy of buildings that reach out to nature with walls of glass, that exemplify shelter with overhanging roofs, that set interior spaces free, and that integrate all components to make each structure a work of art.

Wright's love of nature was instilled in him as a boy in Wisconsin, where he was born on June 8, 1867, in Richland Center. From his father,

a minister and musician, he learned the unity of all things and found that a building could resemble a symphony, "an edifice of sound." From his mother, who gave him a set of educational Froebel blocks at the age of nine, he came to see the inherent geometric structure of nature. In the summer he worked outside on his uncles' farms around Spring Green, where he later made his own home at Taliesin.

But it was the city that called the twenty-year-old Wright, who left his engineering studies at the University of Wisconsin after only one semester and in 1887 became an apprentice in Chicago to Joseph Lyman Silsbee, an architect who was a family friend. A year later, aided by his extraordinary drafting skills, Wright found himself working for Louis Sullivan. One of the most renowned architects of the day, Sullivan became the young draftsman's "Lieber Meister," his revered mentor. The two set out to stem the tide of architectural revivals, Sullivan concentrating on skyscrapers, Wright on the office's residential commissions.

He got his chance to design a house on his own once he and Catherine Lee Tobin married and set up housekeeping in suburban Oak Park in 1889. Their home did not frighten the neighbors—outside it nodded to the popular Queen Anne style even as it launched a revolution inside. Lighted by wide bands of windows, spaces flowed gently to create a sense of vista and spaciousness. The house became an architectural laboratory, as Wright tore down walls and added an avant-garde dining room and playroom for his six children. Six years after leaving Sullivan's employ, the thirty-one-year-old architect built himself a studio attached to his home. Here the barrier between inside and outside began to crumble; the exterior announced the interior's astounding spaces, where an architectural revolution was about to begin.

Wright fortuitously gained the chance to hang out his concrete plaque announcing "Frank Lloyd Wright Architect" after Sullivan let him go in 1892—for designing "bootleg" houses to earn extra income. In these and his first independent houses, designed from 1893 to 1900, he was still exploring what a modern home should look like. Although later in life he asserted that the interior plan dictated all his houses, his changes really began on the outside.

He wanted his clients to avoid anything that "will rear on its hind legs and paw the air in order that you may seem more important than your neighbor." Far better was a house that appeared to grow naturally from its site and harmonize with its surroundings. He recommended unpretentious roofs, sheltering eaves, no porches and front steps but instead a secluded entrance leading to a simple and hospitable front door, walls in earthen hues spreading upward from a substantial base, windows "indicative of good cheer and brightness within." Wright prophesied that his exteriors, more than the interiors, would startle observers, "the result of a radically different conception as to what should constitute a building." At one point he claimed that an early client specified that he did not want a house so different that he would have to slink off to work the back way to avoid his neighbors' laughter.

Although Wright began to simplify the interiors of his new and remodeled houses—reducing confining walls, extending vistas, eliminating applied ornamentation, and building in features to eliminate Victorian clutter—not until the first decade of the twentieth century did he master, and break down, the dichotomy between inside and out. Caring less about what passersby would say, he turned his attention to how people could experience a building inside. The change began with his real-ization that a wall could be more than the side of a box. He began to see walls as enclosures of space, protecting the interior when weather demanded but otherwise free to act as "screens" transmitting light and air.

What these screens looked like outside was determined by the interior plan, itself a response to the needs of people living or working within. In the years when his career reached its first apogee, when he was designing Prairie-style houses from 1910 to about 1917, Wright turned to geometry for his plans. He stretched the popular foursquare layout of the day into freer cruciform and pinwheel plans, all based on standardized unit systems that produced an architectural tapestry woven of inter-dependent units. Respecting the prairie, buildings were low to the ground and repeated materials inside and out for unity and simplicity.

To add interest, surprise, and human scale, he compressed and opened space with differing floor levels, invited views around corners with wood screens, and implied higher ceilings with wood bands and color that brought them down to eye level. The parlor was abandoned in favor of a living room that occupied most of the main floor, with perhaps a "bright, cozy, cheerful" dining room; a fireplace was "the heart of the whole." Basements also disappeared, but the bedrooms were as carefully planned as the living areas. Furnishings were few, with many pieces built in to make "room and furniture 'an entity.'" Textured walls, framed in wood strips, took the place of hanging pictures. Light, in the form of stylized art glass windows, was incorporated into the walls themselves, sifting patterns onto floors like light falling through leaves on a tree.

In the 1920s Wright began to experiment with new materials and new building systems. With four houses in the Los Angeles area, he made a seamless transition from indoors to outdoors, casting concrete into walls

of "textile blocks" that integrated both structure and ornament into their warp and woof. Viewing himself as a weaver, he succeeded in producing a durable fabric as intricately patterned as an oriental rug. Wright continued to explore earth architecture into the 1930s, when he built his Arizona retreat, Taliesin West, out of desert boulders mixed with concrete. Like the California houses, its walls united inside and out by serving both. And at Fallingwater, his legendary 1935 house cantilevered over a waterfall, Wright let the natural setting outside shape the house into a branching tree. Stone walls—including a boulder left in place as the hearth— brought the outdoors into the family's life indoors, just as the house's earthy tans and reds repeated nature's own colors.

Barriers between inside and out diminished further in the mid-1930s, as Wright tried to make houses more affordable for people of average incomes. By devising geometric plans from hexagons to parallelograms, he

molded indoor vistas to avoid right angles. Using generous windows on a house's private side away from the street, he invited in garden views and framed natural landscapes; glass doors offered an easy way to move between interior and exterior worlds. Small spaces were thus made to feel spacious. Nature was tapped for the utilities: heating units buried under red concrete floors simulated the earth, floor-to-ceiling windows captured solar energy, high clerestory windows provided cross-ventilation, and broad roof overhangs created their own shade. Simple board-and-batten cladding or brick used outside came indoors to form walls all of a piece, simplifying construction while simplifying and unifying life inside.

Although Wright designed some four hundred residences—only three-fourths of which were actually built—he had fewer opportunities to turn his hand to places where people work, play, learn, and worship. Yet from his very first structure, he applied the same principles to his public buildings as to his houses. For some of them, such as the Larkin Administration Building, Unity Temple, the S. C. Johnson Administration Building, and the Guggenheim Museum, he had to create his own interior worlds by tuning out distracting environments. His religious structures similarly focused inward but without sacrificing their relationship to nature, Wright's own church. For the Hillside Theater at Taliesin, the Wisconsin home he nurtured over five decades, the architect put the area's pastoral landscape on stage indoors by abstracting it on the theater curtain.

Until his death in 1959, Wright held steadfast to the idea, as he stated in 1931, that the space within was "the great thing to be expressed as architecture. This sense of interior space made exterior as architecture transcended all that had gone before, made all the previous ideas only useful now as a means to the realization of a far greater ideal."

WRIGHT'S OWN HOMES

Houses architects design for themselves are always illuminating peeks into their soul. Wright's are no exception: like Thomas Jefferson, he delighted in putting up only to pull down when a better idea occurred. Wright's three homes—one suburban, one rural, and one desert—reflect responses to three varied sites, needs, and times in his long life. Because his work was so closely woven into his life, none was without its own architectural studio. From the upstairs room in Oak Park where the young architect began working at home to the airy drafting room at Taliesin West, these places ushered in an architectural revolution.

FRANK LLOYD WRIGHT HOME

The first house the twenty-two-year-old architect designed was as much a laboratory for his emerging architectural ideas as it was a home for his growing family. Over two decades Wright moved things around—walls included—to test new concepts as they came to him. On the front a shingled triangle forms an exaggerated gable sheltering a secretive entrance and a projecting bay. In the living room built-in benches nestle into the front and side bays, where walls have vanished in favor of screens of light. "Thus came to an end the cluttered house," said Wright. "Fewer doors; fewer window holes though much greater window area."

1889 | OAK PARK, ILLINOIS

FRANK LLOYD WRIGHT STUDIO

In this studio Wright launched his first golden age. For a decade after he attached a work-place to his home, he and a few associates turned out some 120 Prairie houses that helped change the way people lived. His lifelong fascination with geometry is evident on the approach to the studio: an octagonal library on the right is paired on the left with a two-story drafting room built as an octagon in a square. Designers working on the balcony, which is supported by a chain harness, enjoyed natural light from a band of clerestory windows. Out front, a concrete plaque announced that "Frank Lloyd Wright, Architect," had arrived.

1898 | OAK PARK, ILLINOIS

YE'VE LEFT A GLIMMER STILL TO CHEER
THE MAN ~ THE ARTIFEX
THAT HOLDS IN SPITE O' KNOCKS AND SCALE
O' FRICTION WASTE AN' SLIP,
AN' BY THAT LIGHT ~ NOW MARK MY WORD ~
WE'LL BUILD THE PERFECT SHIP.

TALIESIN

Conceived as a romantic retreat and reworked over a half century, Taliesin held Wright's heart until the end of his days. He built this second home "of the hill," not on it, and found inspiration for the rustic walls in the area's natural rock formations, for the tented ceilings in the nearby hills, and for the sandy tones in the riverbanks below his "shining brow" ("Taliesin" in Welsh). Natural materials and colors ease the transition from outdoors to indoors, making the house at home in nature. In a corner of his personal studio, the architect kept mementos such as a Buddha, dried grass, and a Louis Sullivan panel.

1911 | SPRING GREEN, WISCONSIN

HILLSIDE DRAFTING STUDIO

After the stock market crash of 1929 put clients' projects on hold, Wright decided to become a teacher. In 1932, at the age of sixty-five, he founded the Taliesin Fellowship to share his concept of organic architecture with young apprentices. To house them he converted and expanded the Hillside Home School (designed for his aunts in 1902), adding a low drafting studio connected by a gallery-bridge to the original two-story limestone building. Clerestory windows lining the sawtooth roof filter natural light down into the space around great triangular oak trusses. To Wright it was "an abstract forest" brought inside.

1 9 3 2 | SPRING GREEN, WISCONSIN

OCATILLA

Wright wintered in Arizona for his last twenty-two years, but he first came to know the desert in the 1920s. Called on to design a desert resort, he set up camp in "tents," saying, "We are an outdoor outfit." Canvas roofs alighted like butterflies, according to Wright, atop sand-colored board-and-batten frames. Accents were as rosy as flowers on the ocotillo cactus. Using fifteen buildings—sleeping quarters, living and dining rooms, a kitchen, and a drafting room— Wright designed a resort killed by the Great Depression. Ocatilla burned in 1929, but Wright soon added the desert to his palette.

1929 | PHOENIX, ARIZONA

HILLSIDE THEATER

After Wright created a studio at the Taliesin complex for his new architectural apprentices, he decided to give them a playhouse. The gymnasium of his aunts' old Hillside Home School proved an accommodating space in which students could play in an ensemble or put on a tableau; movies were also shown to the Taliesin family and townspeople. In 1952 a leaf blaze—Taliesin's third fire—destroyed the theater, but it rose again in 1954 in an L shape that puts the audience almost on stage. A curtain of linen and felt uses a geometric language to tell the story of the landscape outside.

1933/1954 | SPRING GREEN, WISCONSIN

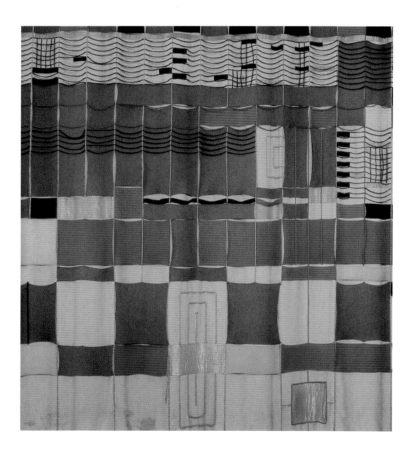

HERE IS THE TEST OF WISDOM ...
WISDOM IS NOT FINALLY TESTED IN
SCHOOLS ... WISDOM CANNOT BE
PASSED FROM ONE HAVING IT TO
ANOTHER NOT HAVING IT .. ..
WISDOM IS OF THE SOUL .. IS NOT
SUSCEPTIBLE OF PROOF. IS ITS OWN
PROOF .. APPLIES TO ALL OBJECTS
STAGES AND QUALITIES . IS CONTENT
WISDOM IS THE CERTAINTY OF THE
REALITY & IMMORTALITY OF THINGS
AND THE EXCELLENCE OF THINGS ..
SOMETHING THERE IS IN THE FLOAT
OF THE SIGHT OF THINGS THAT
PROVOKES IT OUT OF THE SOUL ..

WALT WHITMAN

TALIESIN WEST

When Wright began to build a third home for himself in Arizona, he was finally able to realize a life lived fully outdoors and in—something he could only dream about in Wisconsin winters. The seventy-year-old architect built a new vocabulary from "this great desert-garden": its red floor, its canted mountains, its superbly constructed saguaros, the "dotted lines" of shadows cast by the unrelenting sun. He and the apprentices set desert boulders into concrete for their foundations and topped them with translucent canvas roofs pulled over redwood masts, calling to mind ships on the desert. Life inside was freed to move outside.

1937 | SCOTTSDALE, ARIZONA

TALIESIN WEST DRAFTING ROOM

As Taliesin West was rising up from the desert, the Wrights and the Taliesin Fellowship—
which traveled there from Wisconsin to spend each winter—lived on the property in tents
and simple canvas-and-wood shelters like those at Ocatilla a decade earlier. So that
Wright's architectural work could continue, the second building to be completed was the
drafting room. Its redwood trusses seemed to reach for the mountains nearby, while the
translucent roofs of canvas (now replaced by more permanent materials) barely held the sun
at bay. Being at Taliesin West, said Wright, was like looking down from "the top of the world."

1939 | SCOTTSDALE, ARIZONA

CABARET THEATER

Wright often likened architecture to music, and he was never far from a piano to play. Because he wanted his students also to experience music and theater as part of a well-rounded life, he created entertainment spaces at Taliesin West as he had at Taliesin in Wisconsin. Up the steps past Wright's desert-stone office and behind the cooling fountain, he built an intimate cabaret to replace an earlier dinner theater called the Kiva. Under a flat roof of poured concrete and stone and surrounded by walls of more desert masonry, dinner, music, and a movie were on the weekly bill of fare.

1950 | SCOTTSDALE, ARIZONA

HOMETOWN HOUSES

Like most architects just starting out, Wright found his first clients nearby: around Chicago, where he worked for Louis Sullivan, and Oak Park, where he made his home with his wife, Catherine, and their children. He took commissions as they came, first as an employee of Adler and Sullivan, then moonlighting on the side, and finally on his own. Clients tended to be business people with a progressive outlook, some of whom had architectural visions of their own. Wright's fifty earliest projects are therefore a varied lot that tell more about the era and his patrons than about his own emerging concepts, although they map out changes to come.

CHARNLEY HOUSE

Louis Sullivan was the architect of record for this urban villa, but he preferred designing skyscrapers and so delegated the task to Wright. His young draftsman was eager to try his hand at "as many types of homes as there are types of people." Solids and voids play on the facade, whose stark openings—really holes punched in the wall—telegraph contemporary stripped-down classicism. The exterior's tripartite arrangement clearly expresses the three-part plan inside. Filled with swirls of Sullivanesque ornament that greets visitors right at the front entrance, the wood-lined interiors pay tribute to their client, a lumber magnate.

1891 | CHICAGO, ILLINOIS

PARKER HOUSE

Chronically short of money, Wright undertook a half dozen "bootleg" commissions while working for Sullivan, a transgression that cost him his job—but emboldened him to launch his own practice in 1893. A trio of early houses, sprung from the then-popular Queen Anne style, arose down the street from his own home. In this one the young architect ignored the expected, however, by turning the front tower into an octagon and matching it with another at the rear; by wrapping the tower with generous bands of windows; and by opening up the interior plan. His goal was "to take the starch out of the stiff collar of . . . everyday life. . . ."

1892 | OAK PARK, ILLINOIS

WINSLOW HOUSE

From the street, Wright's first independent commission seemed to nod at tradition with its symmetrical facade, but in reality it was a hybrid of the old and the shockingly new. In the back, the flatness of the golden brick front—sheltered by a taut hat brim of a roof poised over a Sullivanesque frieze—gives way to a semicircular dining room conservatory that pushes the house into nature. Old-fashioned columns frame a bank of windows filled not with the geometric art glass that would become Wright's signature but with delicately etched clear glass. After this house his conception of a house as a "wall-building . . . began to change."

1893 | RIVER FOREST, ILLINOIS

HELLER HOUSE

In this tall house of Roman brick molded to a narrow city lot, Wright finally mastered how to shape space inside and out. A cruciform cube in front holding the living room segues via a broad hall to the dining room in another cube at the back; the entrance in between is reached up a few steps and down a walkway. No longer are the windows mere holes cut out of a wall; they are partners in expressing the space within. "I was working away at the wall as a wall," Wright later recalled, "and bringing it towards the function of a screen." Nymphs in a frieze on the upper loggia dance with pleasure.

1896 | CHICAGO, ILLINOIS

GEORGE FURBECK HOUSE

The year before Wright anchored his new studio with an octagonal library and drafting room, he chose the octagon as the governing spatial motif for a house not far from his own. As a boy he had learned from Froebel blocks to find geometry in nature, and afterward geometry became Wright's architectural language. In the first of two houses designed for brothers, he made the living room an octagon and accentuated the shape with one octagonal tower housing a library and a master bedroom and its pair holding a staircase. Leading into the library are doors of autumnal art glass—a substitute for walls that once confined.

1897 | OAK PARK, ILLINOIS

ROLLIN FURBECK HOUSE

Even as the second of the two Furbeck houses calls to mind the three-part arrangement of the Heller House facade, it presages the Prairie houses to come from Wright's studio. Hipped roofs as broad as the prairie convey the essence of shelter, while high and low exterior forms interpenetrate one another to open up fluid interiors. There wood screens let light and mystery take the place of solid walls and provide built-in ornament of their own. Columns in the central tower offer a more traditional style of ornament, although Wright stylized them with a leaf pattern to show that they came from Oak Park, not Greece.

1897 | OAK PARK, ILLINOIS

PRAIRIE HOUSES

As the twentieth century began, Wright and a number of midwestern architects garnered public acclaim for their efforts to reshape the idea of home. Looking to the flat prairie landscape, Wright designed houses "married to the ground" with broad, sheltering roofs. Seeking simplicity and openness, he eliminated boxy walls. Mirroring nature, he built plans and art glass on geometric foundations. Observing the woods and fields, he chose "the soft, warm, optimistic tones of earth and autumn leaves." Encouraging community, he brought families together around the hearth. By making them works of art, Wright turned houses into homes.

THOMAS HOUSE

One of Wright's first Prairie houses, and the first to go up in Oak Park, was built along the same street as the architect's own shingled home. For Wright, the horizontal was now "the line of domesticity." Over stuccoed, wood-trimmed walls, hipped roofs spread out to reflect the sweep of the prairie. And beneath them, where solid walls used to be, are bands of glittering art glass that make the roofs appear to float. A bower of glass brings nature inside, greeting guests who walk through the archway and ascend a flight of stairs into the shimmering vestibule. "Glass and light—two forms of the same thing!" Wright liked to say.

1901 | OAK PARK, ILLINOIS

WILLITS HOUSE

In creating what Wright regarded as his first great Prairie house, the architect used one of his favorite plans: the cruciform. This cross-shaped arrangement of rooms allowed him to break away from the boxy confines of traditional houses. Gone were small, dark rooms—replaced by indoor "conservatories." Spaces such as the Willitses' dining room, housed in one arm of the cross, were free to invite in light and nature on three sides. Overhead, Wright installed ceiling fixtures that shed soft "moonlight" on the table below. Framed in branching wood bands and dressed in the colors of autumn, the room conjured up a prairie forest.

1902 | HIGHLAND PARK, ILLINOIS

DANA HOUSE

Susan Lawrence Dana—unusual among Wright's clients—had an almost unlimited budget, and he used this freedom to create a masterpiece whose lavishness was never equaled in his seven-decade career. A two-story-tall gallery ringed like a vitrine in art glass is one of a pair of great barrel-vaulted spaces that made this prairie villa an incomparable host; a semicircular window rises over it and the dining room as well. A conservatory walled with some of the hundreds of art glass windows in the house leads back to the entry and reception area. Beneath roofs that seem to flare, a frieze of verdigris plaster adds the final exotic touch.

1902 | SPRINGFIELD, ILLINOIS

HEURTLEY HOUSE

One of Wright's earliest dictums was that a house should appear to grow naturally from its site, so that "you scarcely know where ground leaves off and building begins." He favored brick in earth hues—warm reds, muddy tans, tawny golds—that acknowledge the land on which a building stands. Add a roof that is "a solace to its environment" and you have this house, a good neighbor to Wright's home up the street. The cavelike arch leads to the main living areas upstairs, a plan chosen to take advantage of the best views. A run of geometric art glass windows transformed this urban residence into a Prairie tree house.

1902 | OAK PARK, ILLINOIS

WILLIAM MARTIN HOUSE

Rare because of its height—this is one of only a small handful of Wright's tall Prairie houses—the Martin House is notable even more for the other buildings it launched: William Martin introduced Wright to his brother, Darwin Martin, who became one of the architect's staunchest patrons. Masking the verticality, wood bands outline the stucco facade and slip around corners to create a horizontal counterpoint. In the entrance hall a trellis of art glass overhead and coordinated door panels offer "a thrill of welcome" as Wright liked. The mosaic above the sideboard recalls a garden wonderland outside lost to development.

1902 | OAK PARK, ILLINOIS

DARWIN MARTIN HOUSE

Wright was a wizard with glass, and he used it during the first decade of the twentieth century to furnish his Prairie houses with light, pattern, and color at a single stroke. One of the most beloved of all his glass designs—the Tree of Life—encircles the upper story here just under the broad eaves, transforming the house into a conservatory lined by stylized trees with a geometric yet feathery crown. The metaphor once extended to a real conservatory, reached by way of a glassed-in pergola that invited views of the Martins' elaborate garden. The two were torn down in 1959, leaving Wright's windows to speak for nature.

1904 | BUFFALO, NEW YORK

BEACHY HOUSE

Wright occasionally agreed to remodel an existing house; here virtually nothing of the original escaped his hand. Compared to the more typical hipped roof, a trio of gabled roofs, joined by a veranda projecting into the yard, set a different design course. The contrasting rhythm of brick walls spiced with wood on plaster continues inside, where the dining room picks up the same beat. Oak bands travel up, down, and all around, using what Wright called "eye music" to lower the room to human scale. A lintel-topped fireplace carved from the wall adds warmth to family togetherness.

1906 | OAK PARK, ILLINOIS

COONLEY HOUSE

Family life in this extraordinary suburban villa, as in a number of Wright's Prairie houses, was moved upstairs to the second level to enhance the views outside. Bedrooms were zoned into a cruciform wing creating a court holding servants' quarters and a stable-garage. The living room, nestled under the tented roof, overlooks a large pool that mirrors the house. Its square-patterned windows—together with a custom-designed carpet that once filled the room—reprise a textile-like exterior mosaic woven of rich prairie colors. On either side of the massive brick fireplace ferns originally grew in wall murals that brought nature indoors.

1906 | RIVERSIDE, ILLINOIS

TOMEK HOUSE

A dress rehearsal for Wright's Robie House, this stucco stand-in wears the same features as its more famous relative. Daringly cantilevered roofs punctuated by a squat chimney, ribbons of art glass windows, and flowing interior spaces capped with a bedroom belvedere forecast the Chicago landmark to come from the architect's drawing board two years later. On the main living floor, reached up a stairway from the ground-level entry, a wall of windows stretches past the living room, alongside the dining room, and into a cozy breakfast nook. There more patterned casement windows open outward to take in garden views.

1906 | RIVERSIDE, ILLINOIS

ROBIE HOUSE

With its sweeping cantilevered roofs symbolizing shelter while seeming to defy gravity, the Robie House has come to epitomize Wright's Prairie houses. From the street it appears long, low, and "in league with the ground," but the entrance court shows how adroitly Wright tucked in a third story. The middle level holds the public areas: one continuous space divided by a double fireplace into living and dining sectors. Windows and balcony doors beckon, their patterns providing the privacy of curtains without the obstruction; Wright's motif here incorporates the plan of the house itself.

1908 | CHICAGO, ILLINOIS

ISABEL ROBERTS HOUSE

For design inspiration Wright often looked to trees, seeing in them models for how architecture could grow organically from the earth. In a house for his bookkeeper, he went a step further and incorporated an old elm right into the porch's hipped roof—where it has continued to thrive for nearly a century. At the opposite end of this cruciform plan is a snug dining room, while a two-story living room rises in between. Tall windows filled with diamonds emphasize the height, aided by an encircling balcony that comfortably shares the space. In commissions such as this, Wright succeeded in stifling the boredom of plain walls.

1908 | RIVER FOREST, ILLINOIS

MAY HOUSE

From art glass windows to art glass lamps, from table linens to golden fireplace mortar, this compact house of tawny Roman brick is a prairie symphony with the square its major key. "It is quite impossible," said Wright, "to consider the building one thing and its furnishings another." As he had for a number of recent commissions, he called on the interior designer George Mann Niedecken to help carry out the furnishing plan. Carpets repeat the glass patterns, furniture the autumnal hues of the walls. Before work on this and some other houses was completed, Wright left the country—eager to capture even more adulation abroad.

1908 | GRAND RAPIDS, MICHIGAN

BOYNTON HOUSE

By suggesting early in his career that a dining room need be no more than "a sunny alcove of the living room," Wright forecast the open living spaces that were to become his hallmark. During his Prairie years, however, most clients preferred the formality of a space distinctly set apart for dining. Here Wright gave the widower Edward Boynton a bright alcove as just one of two areas in which to dine. A double bank of art glass windows fills the room with sunshine during the day; at dark, "moonlight" cascades from overhead fixtures. Built-in light standards at the four corners of the table help create the effect of a room within a room.

1908 | ROCHESTER, NEW YORK

STOCKMAN HOUSE

The search for ways to build homes of moderate cost consumed much of Wright's long career. In a proposal published in the *Ladies' Home Journal* in 1907, he assured readers that he could give them "A Fireproof House for $5,000." Wright adapted this design for real-life clients, producing an innovative take on the foursquare house typical of the day. Plain walls were abandoned for a double fireplace that invites movement from the living to the dining area. Wood bands that wrap the stucco exterior come inside as a "deck" running below the ceiling, leading the eye around each room and tying one space to another.

1908 | MASON CITY, IOWA

LAURA GALE HOUSE

"Here is the progenitor of Fallingwater," Wright declared. Although its front terrace and balcony project merely into a secluded street in Oak Park rather than over a rocky waterfall, the house documents Wright's growing ability to mold space. Dark wood trim over light stucco further delineates his daring. Calm prevails inside, where the dining room is set off from the living room by a brief flight of stairs that puts diners at center stage. Built-in bookcases, framed in wood like the exterior, announce the entrance to this inviting retreat. It was all a hint of striking things to come from Wright three decades later.

1909 | OAK PARK, ILLINOIS

STEWART HOUSE

Even in California Wright made the hearth the center of the home. A wall of fire, the brick fireplace climbs up two stories, behind a balcony, to exit at the banded ceiling; a semicircular wall inside the opening radiates heat and adds a soft counterpoint to the strict linearity of the brick mass. Two levels of windows, framed in redwood that branches into a tree pattern, open up the room's other three sides. Wright forsook the brick and stucco he used in the Midwest to clad the exterior in more redwood; boards and battens in this land of sunshine paint the house with light and shadow.

1909 | MONTECITO, CALIFORNIA

IRVING HOUSE

Designed just before Wright departed for Europe with his mistress, Mamah Borthwick Cheney, this expansive Prairie house was among the projects orphaned by the architect's sojourn abroad. Marion Mahony, one of Wright's longtime designers, stepped in to assist, making some architectural modifications and overseeing the furnishings with George Mann Niedecken. These are now gone, but the built-ins remain: banded plaster recalling the facade, wood "decks" joining room to room, and glass etched with a suitably horizontal pattern. Nearby are two houses that Mahony designed on her own.

1909 | DECATUR, ILLINOIS

SECOND LITTLE HOUSE

Francis and Mary Little were two of Wright's repeat clients. A few years after moving into their 1903 Prairie house in Peoria, Illinois, they asked Wright to create a country retreat on the shores of Minnesota's Lake Minnetonka; they waited six years. The architect's grand conception more than repaid their patience. In the living room—intended for private concerts—a crescendo of bold wood bands and delicate art glass rose to a golden skylight, and a Wright-designed table invited displays of Japanese prints. This room was reconstructed at the Metropolitan Museum of Art after the house was inexplicably torn down in 1972.

1912 | WAYZATA, MINNESOTA

BOOTH HOUSE

Wright wanted to create more than single buildings; by 1901 he had in fact sketched out a plan for a neighborhood of Prairie houses. He got his first chance to try his hand at community planning when his attorney, Sherman Booth, asked him to design Ravine Bluffs in the Chicago suburbs. Only five of two dozen houses were completed: one for Booth plus five rentals. Booth rejected a grandiose plan for his own residence, and instead Wright expanded a stable and a garage he had designed in 1912. The addition climbed up to four levels and out to a living room and an adjoining wood-framed porch almost adrift in nature.

1915 | GLENCOE, ILLINOIS

BOGK HOUSE

If this home of narrow Roman brick seems more exotic than the typical Prairie house, it is because Wright was then working on his Imperial Hotel in Tokyo. He had also been fascinated for some time by primitive mesoamerican architecture. For one of his last Prairie commissions, he found a way to combine the monumentality of a Mayan temple with the delicacy of a Japanese screen. Above a two-story light screen of windows, a cast-concrete lintel holding Amerindian chieftains recalls friezes used on his early houses. In the living room the battle of styles gives way to a simple sense of repose.

1916 | MILWAUKEE, WISCONSIN

MIDCAREER HOUSES

Returning from self-imposed exile in Europe and enduring the tragedy of a 1914 fire at Taliesin in which he lost his lover, Wright had to reinvent himself in the 1920s and 1930s. Commissions were scarcer—a mixed blessing that gave him newfound freedom to experiment. In the Los Angeles area he embarked on a "California Romanza," trying out standardized construction systems, learning to build with new materials, and like other modernists exploring primitive motifs that seemed purer and more natural. Soon he became a master teacher, wrote his autobiography, and in his late sixties again showed the world how to build.

HOLLYHOCK HOUSE

Earth, air, fire, and water—Wright brought together the four elements in his hilltop home for the theatrical heiress Aline Barnsdall. For the design, he reached back to "those great American abstractions," the earth buildings of Central America. To savor the California air, he arranged the house around a central courtyard ringed with stylized hollyhocks. To signify home, he built a monumental fireplace whose overmantel dances in geometric steps. And to invite coolness, he planted concentric circles of water at the rear; from a quiet rectangular pond at the front, a small rivulet of water flowed inside to surround the hearth, recombining the elements in one place.

1917 | HOLLYWOOD, CALIFORNIA

LA MINIATURA

As Wright began to experiment in the 1920s with new materials and construction methods, he referred to himself as a weaver. His choice of fabric, however, was unusual: concrete, which he called architecture's "gutter rat." For four houses in the Los Angeles area, he used it to cast so-called textile blocks whose imprints stamped each house with a distinctive integral pattern inside and out. He placed Alice Millard, a widowed former client from Illinois, in a temple that rises out of a ravine like one of its eucalyptus trees. Cross-shaped perforated blocks usher in a daily pageant of light and air, sunshine and shadow.

1923 | PASADENA, CALIFORNIA

STORER HOUSE

Using a trick that had worked to advantage on the prairie—locating the living area on the second story—Wright pushed Dr. John Storer up into the trees for the best views. On the entry level are the bedrooms as well as a large dining room, a kitchen, servants' quarters, and a garage. Above them is a tree house of a living room seemingly hewn from textile blocks, "textured like the trees." At the center a fireplace rises from floor to high ceiling, and on either side terraces make a seamless transition to the outdoors. Patterned and plain, solid and open: concrete wraps the house in a sturdy fabric.

1923 | HOLLYWOOD, CALIFORNIA

FREEMAN HOUSE

For the third of his concrete-block houses, one whose site offered panoramic views, Wright featured another favorite material: glass. To him it was a "magical material, there but not seen," a gift to the modern world that helped destroy boxy classical architecture. Here windows are the yin to the yang of the textile blocks, mirroring their height but shining clear where the blocks are dense, contrasting light with the shadows cast by the concrete. Mitered at the corners, these "blocks" of glass turn walls into a disappearing act. Thanks to Wright's magical material, the outdoors did not have to feel far away.

1923 | LOS ANGELES, CALIFORNIA

ENNIS HOUSE

Wright saw the square as a symbol of integrity; it formed his architectural mark, and he also used it for the last and most monumental of his textile-block houses in Los Angeles. This paean to the exotic pre-Columbian world stretches across its site like a temple high on a hill. Rectilinear columns march in a steadfast row to define a loggia connecting living areas and bedrooms and mediating between indoors and out. On one side they screen views of a pool added by a later owner; from water the loggia leads to fire, contained beneath a golden wisteria mosaic. In the living hall, several steps pirouette up to the dining room.

1923 | LOS ANGELES, CALIFORNIA

WESTHOPE

In a house designed for his cousin Richard Lloyd Jones (the founder of the *Tulsa Tribune)*, Wright returned to the block-and-glass theme of the Freeman House but varied it by letting glass have the lead motif; concrete blocks, mostly plain outside, play second chair. Basking in light behind the front windows, sectioned like the blocks, is a conservatory, but one of the most important interior spaces is outside. A courtyard holding a pool and a fish pond forms an outdoor room—a private place in which to revel in nature. As at Taliesin and elsewhere, Wright directed the family's gaze inward, toward a domestic paradise of its own.

1929 | TULSA, OKLAHOMA

FALLINGWATER

Wright's famous country house for Edgar and Liliane Kaufmann not only opened its arms to nature, it was conceived in the natural world itself. Like a tree taking root near the stream bank, its sandstone trunk shoots up toward the sky; broad concrete terraces branch out into the landscape to catch the sun; and red accents recall autumn leaves. "Go to the woods for your color schemes," Wright admonished as a young architect, following that simple advice here by bringing indoors the same natural materials and colors used outside. Stone walls and floors, brushed with light and shade filtered by clear windows, create their own ornament.

1935 | MILL RUN, PENNSYLVANIA

WINGSPREAD

In a descriptively named house for Herbert F. Johnson, four wings literally spread outward in pinwheel fashion from a central "wig-wam" spiraling up three stories. Octagonal tiers of clerestories wrap around an elliptical fireplace whose individual openings warm living, dining, and library nooks in the grand hall; furnishings repeat the geometric theme. The wings reach out in different directions for different activities: the master suite, children's rooms (by the pool), guest rooms, and servants' quarters and the kitchen. Wright saw this as his last Prairie house, but in truth it ushered in a new way of building.

1937 | RACINE, WISCONSIN

USONIAN HOUSES

In the midst of the Great Depression in the 1930s, Wright turned his attention to creating "the house of moderate cost"—the country's greatest architectural problem, he said. Naming them Usonian after the United States of North America, he came up with smaller, more open homes suitable to a more relaxed way of life. He used a unit system and geometric modules to simplify design, sandwiched walls to trim construction costs, combined living and dining areas but sequestered bedrooms in a "quiet zone," moved the heating underfoot, and brought the outdoors inside—all "to liberate the people living in the house."

FIRST JACOBS HOUSE

Fresh from designing homes for scions of industry, Wright started searching for ways to house teachers and journalists with the same care but at lower cost. His solution was to simplify: not just the building systems and the number and types of materials but also the lives of clients such as Katherine and Herbert Jacobs. "Mr. and Mrs. Jacobs," he said, "must themselves see life in somewhat simplified terms. . . ." He gave them his first Usonian, an L-shaped residence that turned a quiet face to the street while opening up on the private side. Windows in place of walls add a sense of spaciousness and vista to a compact yet liberating space.

1936 | MADISON, WISCONSIN

HANNA HOUSE

California's casual lifestyle spurred Wright in his quest for simpler ways of living. For his clients Paul and Jean Hanna he noted how bees build and spun out his own "honeycomb house." Hexagonal spaces lie atop a hexagonal grid, eliminating the psychic restrictions of right-angle rooms. The living room hearth inside and the pavers outside gently reinforce the overriding plan. This is an indoor-outdoor house, surrounded by patios reached by folding glass doors that do their part to carry out the theme. It provided, the Hannas later reflected, "a perpetual ringside seat at the great performances of nature."

1936 | STANFORD, CALIFORNIA

JESTER-PFEIFFER HOUSE

The next geometric motif to capture Wright's curiosity was the circle—a symbol of infinity—with which he had begun to play in earlier windows and murals. For a client's coastal site in California, he offered up balloons brought to earth under a flat roof: a series of separate disks framed in bent plywood. Neither Ralph Jester nor nine other clients built the house until 1971, when it was adapted in stucco for the desert just beyond Taliesin West by Bruce Brooks Pfeiffer, now Wright's archivist. Each living pavilion opens onto a meandering red patio, requiring movement from indoors to outdoors to go from room to room.

1938/1971 | SCOTTSDALE, ARIZONA

POPE-LEIGHEY HOUSE

Labor had grown too costly to handcraft art glass windows for his Usonian houses, so the architect devised a more streamlined way of incorporating pattern. Wood panels perforated in inventive geometric shapes—some of them mirroring the plan of the house itself—were installed inside and out. Used in high clerestory windows, the built-in cutouts stenciled sunny messages on walls and floors. Loren Pope, a journalist, sought out such a house from Wright, who responded with a doll-sized home whose two bedrooms are reached down a narrow hall. Perforated-plywood boards sift natural light into the house to guide the way.

1939 | ALEXANDRIA, VIRGINIA

GOETSCH-WINCKLER HOUSE

In this house for two college educators, wooden cutouts were forsaken for ceiling-high clerestories of clear glass that raise the roof up into the trees. They mark the house's public side, while an adjacent bank of tall windows opens the living area to its wooded site. The built-in dining table is a buffer between the efficient "workspace" (as Wright called his kitchens) and the living room—studio, with its alcove and fireplace. Two bedrooms front on a lanai, expanding the house outdoors. The straight-line plan is punctuated by a deeply cantilevered carport, a Wright invention that housed the modern car as efficiently as its driver.

1939 | OKEMOS, MICHIGAN

ROSENBAUM HOUSE

The carport of this college professor's home points the way inside while it energizes the plain brick face the house turns to the street. As with other Usonians, the windows are found indoors, along the living room wall that announces the garden terrace. To supplement the natural light, ceiling fixtures of perforated wood shed illumination as well as pattern over the dining corner. Gone are the formal dining rooms favored by Wright's businessman clients at the turn of the twentieth century; in their place came tables angled into the masonry core holding the fireplace, the utilities, and the petite "workspace" devoted to meal preparation.

1939 | FLORENCE, ALABAMA

STURGES HOUSE

After Fallingwater, this is Wright's most dramatic tree house. Like a number of his Prairie and Usonian designs, it rises *en pointe* to frame picturesque views—in this case, the city of Los Angeles spread out below. Lapped redwood boards conceal a terrace that wraps around the living room and two bedrooms, increasing the tiny house's 870 square feet of living space both visually and actually. Overhead a trellis becomes a sun umbrella; punched with squares repeating the house's module, it traces its patterns on the deck below. Wright's plywood chairs are at home in this interior forest.

1939 | BRENTWOOD HEIGHTS, CALIFORNIA

AULDBRASS PLANTATION

On a site barely above a low-lying swampland populated by cypress trees and live oaks webbed with Spanish moss, Wright clearly let nature inspire him. Tidewater cypress walls in this modern-day plantation sway inward like wind-blown trees, their clear glass traced with wood patterns that emulate branches. A beamed canopy in the living room of the main house, which is designed on a hexagonal plan, heightens the effect of walking in the woods; high clerestory windows filter leafy dappled light into the room. By the pool, a pergola serves as one of several indoor-outdoor spaces that recall antebellum ways of building.

1939 | YEMASSEE, SOUTH CAROLINA

OBOLER RETREAT

Even tinier than the Sturges House, Eleanor Oboler's hilltop aerie makes up in view what it lacks in size. This one-room studio designed for the wife of the radio and movie personality Arch Oboler turns west to lock in its sights the majestic purple mountains that overlook the Pacific Ocean. Rubblestone masonry that Wright used at Taliesin West reappears here to anchor the retreat to its perch. Although a large estate was planned, only this little lookout and a gatehouse complex where the Obolers lived were completed. Like many commissions that came Wright's way, the dreams were easier to visualize than to realize.

1940 | MALIBU, CALIFORNIA

AFFLECK HOUSE

Gregor and Elizabeth Affleck were two of many clients who came to Wright after being inspired by Fallingwater. Although not as resplendent, their site included a ravine cut through by a stream. Wright raised this house of lapped cypress and brick so that its living room and terrace project into the landscape like its model. Opposite the entry a glassed-in loggia, shaded by a deep trellis, invites views of the wooded setting from floor-to-ceiling doors; a skylight frames the treetops. And, again recalling Fallingwater, a well open to the stream below interjects the sight and sound of water.

1941 | BLOOMFIELD HILLS, MICHIGAN

SECOND JACOBS HOUSE

To his search for economical ways of building Wright added the hope of energy efficiency. He disliked air conditioning, preferring clerestory windows for cross-ventilation and roof overhangs for shade. In his second house for the Jacobs family he devised the first of his "solar hemicycles": passive solar houses with concave walls cupped to scoop up the sun. Here an earth berm against the stone wall offers shelter on the north, while on the south both the living areas and the bedrooms above drink in the warmth of the solar rays. A caldera carved into the earth beyond the terrace serves as a garden and completes the circular motif.

1944 | MIDDLETON, WISCONSIN

CEDAR ROCK

Water brought out the best in Wright, who saw it as nature's mirror. For this river bend, he responded with a mirror of his own: glass. A prototype for a house published in the *Ladies' Home Journal* proved ready made for Lowell and Agnes Walter's waterfront property. In the living area—called a "garden room"—window walls, high clerestories, and square skylights pull in sunshine to feed the greenery as well as views to nourish the soul. Finished in 1950, after wartime material shortages, the house and its riverside boathouse used costlier brick and ushered in more substantial Usonians.

1945 | QUASQUETON, IOWA

MELVYN SMITH HOUSE

Some clients still had to keep a close eye on their budgets. A number of them became their own contractors—and even builders—so they could afford the Wright house of their dreams. With its L-shaped, board-and-batten design, Sara and Melvyn Maxwell Smith's plan harked back to the earliest Usonians. Melvyn, a teacher, searched out the best bargain on tidewater cypress. Its golden tones warm the living area and flow into the dining alcove, lighted by an arbor of perforated plywood. As the family grew, so did the house; the bedroom wing was expanded just as Wright had allowed for.

1946 | BLOOMFIELD HILLS, MICHIGAN

ALBERT ADELMAN HOUSE

Throughout his career Wright kept returning to concrete, architecture's "outcast." For this house near Milwaukee he used it plain rather than mold it with varied patterns as he had in California in the 1920s. Concrete blocks form walls inside as well as outside, where they are stepped to add rhythm and shadow. A long cloistered gallery, as Wright called his hallways, leads from the entry to three bedrooms all in a row; its sense of seclusion is relieved only by compact windows and a cathedral ceiling of cypress beams. At the house's opposite end, another gallery—as open as this is closed—connects the living and dining rooms.

1946 | FOX POINT, WISCONSIN

MOSSBERG HOUSE

Like the Prairie houses before them, the Usonians lie close to the ground, many of them with flat roofs underscoring their horizontality. In others, such as this, Wright raised the roof to achieve an equally effective symbol of shelter. Wood bands emphasize the living room's two-story height; a mezzanine outside an upstairs bedroom extends the vista toward the far side of the house. An asymmetrical fireplace of brick to match the exterior cladding draws the eye to the room's focal point. Around the corner, the dining area and the kitchen, which rises upward to the second story, capture space outside through terrace doors of clear glass.

1948 | SOUTH BEND, INDIANA

SOL FRIEDMAN HOUSE

In the early 1930s Wright had begun to flesh out his ideas for "wedding ... the city and the country" in democratic settlements of organic architecture generically called Broadacre City. He was given several chances to remake the American landscape to fit his vision, but none was ever completed. Only three Wright-designed houses rose at Usonia Homes, where he had sketched out fifty-five circular lots of an acre each. Pie-shaped like the plan, this house simulates a rocky outcropping with exaggerated slits for windows. To the south, a wall of glass welcomes the sun as a guest at the table.

1948 | PLEASANTVILLE, NEW YORK

ERIC BROWN HOUSE

Parkwyn Village in Kalamazoo was another of Wright's planned Usonian communities; here four of the houses—out of forty-one envisioned on circular lots—were his. Eric and Ann Brown's residence on Taliesin Drive is another exploration of concrete block built with a simple in-line plan placing the bedrooms in their own "quiet zone." Its watery hearth offers an indoor garden and recalls the moated fireplace at Hollyhock House. As in most Usonians, the simple plywood furnishings fit the house's geometry as well as a variety of needs. Wright disliked paintings tacked onto a wall, so he built in shelves to allow changing shows.

1949 | KALAMAZOO, MICHIGAN

WALKER HOUSE

For Wright the site was the beginning of architecture. The earth—and sometimes the sea—dictated how his organic buildings would grow. Monterey Bay called for a ship of stone as sandy as the shore with a copper roof as green as the water. The prow holds a deck-like terrace sheltering a hexagonal living-dining space. A built-in sofa commands views out tiered windows that open downward to avoid gusts; Cherokee red, Wright's signature color, adds an earthy counterpoint to the clear glass. It was all "a *natural* performance, . . . integral to site . . . to environment . . . to the life of the inhabitants."

1949 | CARMEL, CALIFORNIA

LAURENT HOUSE

The solar hemicycle plan used in the second Jacobs House reappeared in another midwestern town where sun needs to be coaxed indoors year-round. This time a terrace and a garden scribe the convex side to complete an elliptical shape holding an elliptical pool. Inside, a narrow garden room is molded to the concave curve of the glass wall overlooking the terrace. Built-in seating saves precious space and reinforces the room's geometry, while built-in cabinets keep freestanding furniture to a minimum. Two bedrooms open off the main living area, offering one-level living to the disabled owner.

1949 | ROCKFORD, ILLINOIS

DAVID WRIGHT HOUSE

To escape the heat of the desert floor, Wright devised a raised prototype called "How to Live in the Southwest" and adapted it for his son David's property in the midst of a citrus grove. Essentially a solar hemicycle, the concrete-block design turns into a circle thanks to a spiraling ramp that sweeps skyward. Cylinders on the sides house the kitchen, utilities, and fireplaces. Filling the center at ground level is a garden court visible from windows lining the inner curve; along the outer perimeter, more windows open onto a balcony. Half-moon windows, a rotund fireplace, and a rug bubbling with circles reinforce the motif inside.

1950 | PHOENIX, ARIZONA

PALMER HOUSE

Marked on the polished red concrete floor for all to see, the triangle is clearly in charge here. Mary and William Palmer's combined living-dining room occupies one large equilateral triangle whose third point is completed outside by the terrace. Three bedrooms rest in two other interlocking triangles, one of them completed by a triangular study. Underfoot is Wright's gravity heating system, conceived to eliminate radiators in favor of imbedded hotwater pipes that suffuse warmth as if it were rising from the earth. Pierced brick outside is reprised inside. For a couple who loved music as much as he, Wright created a symphony.

1950 | ANN ARBOR, MICHIGAN

ZIMMERMAN HOUSE

This is a small house made to look and feel large—Wright's secret formula. A dramatically cantilevered carport unfurls near the entrance to balance the extended living-dining wing. Inside, an asymmetrical fireplace attracts attention by rising as high as the gabled roof allows; both its red brick and its masonry lintel neatly repeat the materials used outside. Tucked away behind this natural room divider is the dining alcove set beside a wall of glass. This private side of the house contrasts with its public facade, where nothing but small square windows set into a frieze interrupts the interior repose.

1950 | MANCHESTER, NEW HAMPSHIRE

BERGER HOUSE

Devotion to Wright's ideals plus many years of hard work paid Robert and Gloria Berger's admission into the select coterie of homeowners who did it themselves to get a Wright house. Robert, an engineering teacher, mixed stone and concrete to produce a rustic masonry directly descended from the architect's own Taliesin West. Rubblestone walls define the exterior perimeters and come indoors to tie the house to the earth. A great stone fireplace occupies a masonry core embodying the living area's hexagonal form. From a floor as red as clay to the ceiling evoking a forest, the house wears the colors and textures of nature.

1950 | SAN ANSELMO, CALIFORNIA

REISLEY HOUSE

Where the Friedman House, the first of Wright's designs for the Usonia Homes community, took the circle as its form, the third of his three houses there used a triangle plan that infused many of the Usonians with uncommon energy. Despite the hilly site, the plan accommodated an expansion in 1956 that added three bedrooms and a playroom. Wright regarded his houses as organic—always growing—and called the Usonians "polliwogs" whose tail length depended on the number of children to be housed. In this house of cypress and granite, Roland and Ronny Reisley raised a family and have stayed on for a half century.

BENJAMIN ADELMAN HOUSE

Pursuing his belief that a house might be made so simple that it could almost build itself, in the 1950s Wright developed a system he called Usonian Automatics. Concrete block became the material as well as the unit measure on which these residences were constructed, without union labor, thereby eliminating one budget item. Acknowledging Arizona's climate, this house—renovated and expanded in the 1980s—was designed as two units linked by a covered breezeway facing a garden court. Concrete walls provide an unassuming backdrop for a living room mural by Eugene Masselink, one of Wright's closest apprentices.

1951 | PHOENIX, ARIZONA

BRANDES HOUSE

While promoting the idea that each house should grow from its own site, Wright liked to revive and reinvent successful house plans. For the builder Ray Brandes and his wife, Mimi, the architect reached back more than a decade and adapted the design of the Goetsch-Winckler House in concrete block to suit this large wooded property. A red concrete mat encircles the house, leading to the door and on inside in one unifying stroke of color. Windows, French doors, and two tiers of clerestories in the living area draw in as much light as possible; the three bedrooms use glass and a terrace to extend themselves into outdoor rooms.

1952 | ISSAQUAH, WASHINGTON

ROBERT L. WRIGHT HOUSE

One son received a circle in the desert, another—the youngest, an attorney known as Llewellyn—an ellipse overlooking a ravine in suburban Washington, D.C. Wright's mastery of concrete block is evident at the front door, where solids and voids tango on the curving walls. The second-story perforations bring light into the upstairs gallery leading to the bedrooms. Inside the cylinder are the kitchen and a circular hearth at ground level and a bathroom and second fireplace above. The private side of the house, sided in wood, opens to the landscape in two tiers of floor-to-ceiling windows.

1953 | BETHESDA, MARYLAND

USONIAN PAVILION

At the age of eighty-six, when his international exhibition *Frank Lloyd Wright: Sixty Years of Living Architecture* stopped in New York City, Wright was able to share his ideas about the modern home with an audience much larger than his several hundred clients. A temporary Usonian house went up on the present site of Wright's Guggenheim Museum, allowing visitors an unparalleled opportunity to tour his concept of home. The free-flowing, airy living-dining space was furnished with Wright designs. Although the house was dismantled the next year, its open plan came back to life in several later designs in Iowa and Ohio.

1953 | NEW YORK, NEW YORK

TONKENS HOUSE

One of the most luxurious of the Usonian Automatics, located outside Cincinnati, relies on so many open blocks that it seems to be a basket woven of concrete. Blocks inset with glass paint sun-and-shadow patterns in the living-dining space and the bedrooms arranged in line at the opposite end. Because most Usonian kitchens are set into the core of the house with no outside exposure except a skylight here or there, the Tonkens "workspace" is exceptional: it pulls in light from both the terrace facade and an elevated clerestory atop the cabinets. Wright changed the housewife from a "kitchen-mechanic" to a scientist in her laboratory.

1954 | AMBERLEY VILLAGE, OHIO

HAROLD PRICE SR. HOUSE

Wright's "obedient servant," concrete, put in a star performance in this desert oasis for the Oklahoma oilman who commissioned the Price Tower. In the central entrance atrium, pyramid-stepped columns of concrete block surround a cooling fountain under a roof partially open to the sky; doors by Eugene Masselink can be closed when storms threaten, and a saw-toothed fireplace offers warmth. Turn right to enter the living-dining area, the kitchen, and the guest wing across a loggia. Turn left into a long gallery, and an in-line dormitory for visitors awaits beside a patio and pool. Its hospitality garnered it the nickname Grandma House.

1954 | PHOENIX, ARIZONA

KENTUCK KNOB

Layered sandstone walls and flagstone flooring are reminders of Wright's most famous Pennsylvania house, Fallingwater, but here he gave his client Isaac Hagan a stone steamer that steers toward a view of land, not water. The single-story residence snakes along its site in a parallelogram, a typical Usonian plan, overlaid with hexagonal and triangular modules. Hexagonal cutouts turn the copper roof into a trellis over a terrace enveloping the living area. Just beyond a projecting stone fireplace, in a sunny corner beside the landlocked kitchen, a handcrafted table by George Nakashima filled the dining alcove before a fire.

1954 | CHALKHILL, PENNSYLVANIA

TRACY HOUSE

For yet another Usonian Automatic, its site across Puget Sound inspired Wright to build in plenty of view. Mitered-glass insets are woven into perforated concrete blocks along the living room terrace, where simple glass doors bring the outdoors in naturally. The delicacy of the block-and-glass columns is a foil for the coffered blocks that form the ceiling and the fireplace, which steps down below floor level. Beyond the dining nook is the kitchen and three bedrooms along a gallery. Despite Wright's fond desire that these houses build themselves, most homeowners had to rely on professional assistance and oversight by Taliesin.

1 9 5 5 | S E A T T L E , W A S H I N G T O N

RAYWARD HOUSE

Concrete and water mix here to produce a consummate solar hemi-cycle whose pools and pond reflect its originality. A glass arc on the concave side acts as a sun catcher, while a poolside terrace completes the elliptical line outdoors. Philippine mahogany frames the windows and then branches upward across the ceiling. Clustered along the window wall are the living and dining spaces, where built-in cabinets hide the kitchen. Garden doors and high clerestories opposite supplement the light. Wings hold such delights as a bedroom observatory, an elliptical playhouse, and a bomb shelter.

1955 | NEW CANAAN, CONNECTICUT

PETERSON COTTAGE

Wright felt challenged by every housing need, even that of a young would-be Taliesin apprentice. A year before his death, the architect produced what has been called "more architecture per square foot [880] than any building Wright ever built." Above a terrace wall of rusticated sandstone, branching wood panels trace the upward rise of the shed roof. The one-room interior is divided into living, cooking, sleeping, and bathing areas by a fireplace that echoes the exterior materials. After Seth Peterson took his life before moving in, the lakeside cottage fell into decay but has been restored and now welcomes paying guests.

1958 | LAKE DELTON, WISCONSIN

LOVNESS COTTAGE

Donald and Virginia Lovness are two of the devoted clients who decided in 1955 that if they were to have a Wright house they could afford, they would have to build it themselves. They hauled limestone for the walls of their lakefront home, assembled the furniture, and did the upholstery themselves. In 1958 Wright drew up plans for several cottages; the one that was finally built is a cousin to the Peterson Cottage, which shares a similar lake view and North Woods climate. To furnish their cottage, the Lovnesses revived Wright's unexecuted drawings for a whimsical dining set created for Aline Barnsdall at Hollyhock House.

1958/1972 | STILLWATER, MINNESOTA

ABLIN HOUSE

Like tea leaves, the plan of this house can be read in the parallelograms cross-hatched on its red concrete floormat. Etched in wood, the same geometry marks the windows that project the living room's triangular prow onto the terrace. Designed in the last full year of Wright's life, Millie and George Ablin's concrete-block residence was enlarged somewhat on the final drawings completed after the architect's death. Five bedrooms and a study fill wings on either side of the main living space. Its chairs and tables, built to Wright's specifications and hues, reflect the plan itself and work together as vital parts of the architecture.

1958 | BAKERSFIELD, CALIFORNIA

STROMQUIST HOUSE

Concrete block, a parallelogram plan, parallelograms bisected into great triangular prows, all sheltered by a cantilevered roof—Wright took elements that had built his legacy over the past two decades and reshuffled them once again for a masterful home placed in a canyon high above the Great Salt Lake. Except for the kitchen set into the house's core, right angles fail to make an appearance. Even the gridded windows in the living room angle subtly away from the walls, meeting at one point in a mitered corner. In the ceiling, inset with triangular lights, wood bands extend from the mullions like ribbons, tying together the unified plan.

1958 | BOUNTIFUL, UTAH

CRIMSON BEECH

Wright, who had explored prefabrication as early as 1915, turned to it again in 1956 as a way to make Usonia more affordable. He teamed up with the developer Marshall Erdman to produce several models that *House and Home* promoted as "the biggest news for 1957." For their site with a venerable copper beech tree, William and Catherine Cass ordered an in-line prefab with a carport and family room. Board-and-batten from the facade and brick used on the rear walls reappear inside. But the $55,000 price tag put even these streamlined Usonians beyond middle-class budgets.

1959 | STATEN ISLAND, NEW YORK

LYKES HOUSE

The ninety-one-year-old architect had time to do little more than sketch out his idea for this hilly site before he died on April 9, 1959. Perhaps thinking of infinity he chose the circle, giving Aime and Norman Lykes two towers from which to watch Phoenix grow. The first holds the living-dining space and a perfect circle of a kitchen, which looks out onto a circular garden court through semicircular portholes. A slim gallery curves past the bedrooms toward the master bedroom in the second tower. Built of man-made concrete block, the house swirls up as naturally from the ground as if it had just grown there.

1959 | PHOENIX, ARIZONA

PUBLIC BUILDINGS

Although Wright was above all an architect of houses, he designed everything from museums to a beer hall to at least one dog house—or from cathedrals to chicken coops, as he bragged. The opportunity to create more public buildings, especially government structures, would have suited him, but such sponsors proved more timid than his residential clients. Wright nonetheless reshaped the world of office work with the Larkin and S. C. Johnson Company Buildings, churches with Unity Temple and the Unitarian Meeting House, and art appreciation with a spiral in New York City that turned museum going upside down.

LARKIN ADMINISTRATION BUILDING

Given the opportunity by Darwin Martin to design the headquarters of a mail-order soap and home products company, Wright decided to focus the Larkin Building inward. Turning away from a characterless industrial site, it created its own interior world. A skylight became its sky, showering sunshine into an atrium ringed by open galleries whose brick trunks branched up into geometric capitals. Mechanical systems and stairs were moved to the corners to free up the building's center. But like a number of Wright's most astounding public spaces, the Larkin Building had a short life—falling in 1950 to make way for a parking lot.

1 9 0 3 | B U F F A L O , N E W Y O R K

UNITY TEMPLE

It was this commission that led Wright to prove that "the enclosed space within . . . is the *reality* of the building." Inside needs—for an unencumbered space holding "the sky pilot on the floor with his flock"—dictated the outer form. Load-bearing posts moved inward to create a pavilion: a roof cantilevered above bands of art glass windows. Skylights in the coffered ceiling convey the "sense of a happy cloudless day," lighted by miniature suns posing as lamps. Beyond the pulpit and organ screen the entrance loggia leads to the parish house, encased economically like the main cube in reinforced concrete as naked and taut as skin.

1904 | OAK PARK, ILLINOIS

COONLEY PLAYHOUSE

Like the Martin family, the Coonleys of Riverside, Illinois, were among the satisfied Wright clients who returned to him for multiple projects. Queene Coonley, a proponent of progressive education, went to her progressive architect when she decided to build a school, called a playhouse. On a stage in one arm of its cruciform plan children were encouraged to try out their dramatic skills. At the opposite end of the cross lies a trio of windows that a playful Wright pulled out of his imagination to conjure up the balloons, confetti, and flags of a parade. The same childlike motifs and colors march above in high clerestory windows.

1912 | RIVERSIDE, ILLINOIS

MIDWAY GARDENS

Lost to us far longer than it was around to provide pleasure—it was torn down in 1929—Midway Gardens was probably Wright's most joyous composition. It was meant to be Chicago's answer to the outdoor restaurants and beer halls of Europe, but the developer went bankrupt in 1916. While the fun lasted, crowds enjoyed the Summer Garden outdoors or moved indoors to the Winter Garden; a band shell encouraged dancing. Walls of yellow brick were woven with abstract cast-concrete motifs, attenuated sprites guarded the court, and murals danced with circles, all together producing a symphony of sights and sounds.

1913 | CHICAGO, ILLINOIS

IMPERIAL HOTEL

Other than nature, the only inspiration Wright ever acknowledged was Japanese culture: its temples, its woodblock prints, its golden screens. The Japanese honored him with four commissions, including his masterwork—this famed hotel, which rode out an earthquake on its opening day in 1923. Guest rooms along the sides of the H-shaped structure were linked to public spaces through long promenades, where blocks of oya (lava stone, also used outside) were carved into exotic motifs. War, inattention, and economics spurred the landmark's demise in 1968, but the lobby and reflecting pool were later rebuilt at an outdoor museum.

1915 | TOKYO, JAPAN

S. C. JOHNSON ADMINISTRATION BUILDING

Although this renowned office building creates its own interior world like the Larkin Building, it is as rounded and streamlined as the earlier structure was hard-edged. Light is allowed into the three-story Administration Building through rifts in its red brick walls filled with Wright's innovative alternative to plain windows: translucent Pyrex glass tubing. Emphasizing the building's horizontality, rivulets of light rain down from clerestories, encase an arched passage, and bubble up in the reception area. More glass tubing in the fifteen-story Research Tower added later merges smoothly with the brick to produce a sleek exclamation mark.

1936 | RACINE, WISCONSIN

FLORIDA SOUTHERN COLLEGE

The first building Wright designed for the campus of this Methodist college was its chapel. As he had begun to do at Unity Temple, this son and grandson of ministers continued to reshape archetypes—he called them clichés—of what religious buildings should look like. Where a steeple might have been, he placed a windowed bell tower that fills the Pfeiffer Chapel with light as well as sound. A choir loft filigreed in a hexagonal concrete pattern mimicks the building's plan. Concrete blocks made from sand and coquina shells reflect the bright sunshine outdoors, where covered esplanades become umbrellas linking the buildings.

1938–54 | LAKELAND, FLORIDA

UNITARIAN MEETING HOUSE

All pretense of a steeple has vanished in this church, whose triangular form touches the sky like prayerful hands. Soaring above walls of stacked limestone, the copper roof cloaks a window that projects the triangular theme outward. Mirrored by a great stone fireplace at one end of the auditorium, a stone core holds the pulpit beneath the choir's balcony. At dark, starry lights twinkle in the plaster ceiling above. All of a piece, it symbolized unity for Wright, who was raised a Unitarian, and "says what the steeple used to say, but says it with greater reverence . . . in both form and structure."

1947 | MADISON, WISCONSIN

MORRIS GIFT SHOP

Inset square lights—not showy plate-glass windows—lead the way to the door of this intimate store. An arched tunnel of narrow Roman brick signifies that the goal has been reached. When Wright was called in to remodel this shop, he had been at work for five years on the Guggenheim Museum in New York City (and it would not be completed until after his death in 1959). Circles were thus on his mind, and the exaggerated arch at the door is just the first of many that await inside. In the center a ramp spirals upward past displayed wares toward a celestial ceiling of bulbous glass clouds.

1948 | SAN FRANCISCO, CALIFORNIA

FIRST CHRISTIAN CHURCH

Another church, designed as the chapel of the Southwest Christian Seminary, languished on the drawing boards for two decades until it was revived after the architect's death. Here a spire inset with glass miraculously reappears, but it is more than a symbol of aspiration. Rising from a spine of clerestory windows, it is an outward manifestation of inner light— Wright himself saw it as a lantern. Only the congregants are privy to the stained glass panels lining the clerestories. The openness of the glassed-in sides enhances the feeling of being in a tent, albeit one tied to the ground with desert masonry under a simulated copper roof.

PRICE TOWER

In 1956 Wright sketched out a mile-high skyscraper for Chicago, but this nineteen-story tower on the prairie (based on the unexecuted 1929 design for St. Mark's Tower in New York City) was his tallest building. To Wright it was "a tree that escaped the forest." From a trunk at center, reinforced-concrete floors branch out in a pinwheel to hold offices and eight two-story apartments. Exterior walls have become screens with copper panels, shaded by copper louvers and gold-tinted glass. Metallic finishes extend to the office of Harold Price Sr., furnished with cast-aluminum chairs and a Wrightian mural.

1952 | BARTLESVILLE, OKLAHOMA

ANDERTON COURT SHOPS

Shoppers out looking for diamonds on Rodeo Drive can find the architectural kind in this faceted arcade based on Wright's favorite diamond: the parallelogram. As at the Morris Gift Shop and the Guggenheim Museum, a ramp draws visitors in and upward to six shops and a penthouse staggered at half levels on three floors; one was intended originally as a residence. Portholes open onto the inside passage that runs from the central court to the rear. Rising overhead is a serrated tower cast in fiberglass, a compelling beacon recalling the First Christian Church's lighted spire and the Marin County Civic Center's signature tower.

1952 | BEVERLY HILLS, CALIFORNIA

BETH SHOLOM SYNAGOGUE

In contrast to the Christian Trinity symbolized by his triangular design for the Unitarian Meeting House, for this synagogue Wright went to Mount Sinai. A mountain of light, clothed in glass outside and fiberglass inside, envelops the main sanctuary. A thousand congregants, segregated into triangular seating segments that mirror the building plan, can fill the great hall, facing the Ark holding the Torah. More triangles float overhead in the rainbow-colored chandelier, the concrete soffit, and the ceiling superstructure. Along the ridges of the roof, seven abstracted menorahs add their own light.

1954 | ELKINS PARK, PENNSYLVANIA

KUNDERT MEDICAL CLINIC

For the ophthalmology clinic of two doctors from Wisconsin, Wright turned to a residential idiom as a means of putting patients at ease. Features drawn from his Usonian houses are clear: a one-story L-shaped plan, perforated-wood designs in the waiting room, even a hearth to signify domestic security. A triple stack of mahogany clerestories rises above the building's flat roof to bring in cheer, while glass doors just past the fireplace extend the view to a triangular terrace. The forest-like palette is enhanced by red brick whose mortar is tinted to achieve seamless color and a red concrete floor incised with the clinic's square module.

1954 | SAN LUIS OBISPO, CALIFORNIA

DALLAS THEATER CENTER

No stranger to theatricality himself, Wright relished the challenge of designing a theater—although only a few of his designs were built. The Hillside Theatre at Taliesin incorporated his opinion that "the proscenium was a thing of the past." For the Kalita Humphreys Theater in Dallas, he similarly brought the show to the people, lowering the stage to join actors and audience in a circular embrace. The forty-foot round stage rests in a concrete drum that rises above the building to serve as its marquee. Here architecture's most famous showman produced a theater in which players and audience are "sympathetically related to each other as one."

1955 | DALLAS, TEXAS

GUGGENHEIM MUSEUM

In Wright's eyes a spiral—evolving in a continuous stream—epitomized the idea of organic architecture. Although a 1924 ziggurat planned for a Maryland mountaintop never saw the light of day, he persevered over sixteen years, from 1943 to 1959, to see a similar vision materialize on Fifth Avenue. Swirls of concrete outside announce the interior landscape: one continuous floor surface beneath an indoor sky that unfurls works of art from top to bottom. As if it were plastic, Wright molded his material into a museum as abstract as the art it was designed to display. Based on his revised plan of 1956, it finally opened after his death.

1956 | NEW YORK, NEW YORK

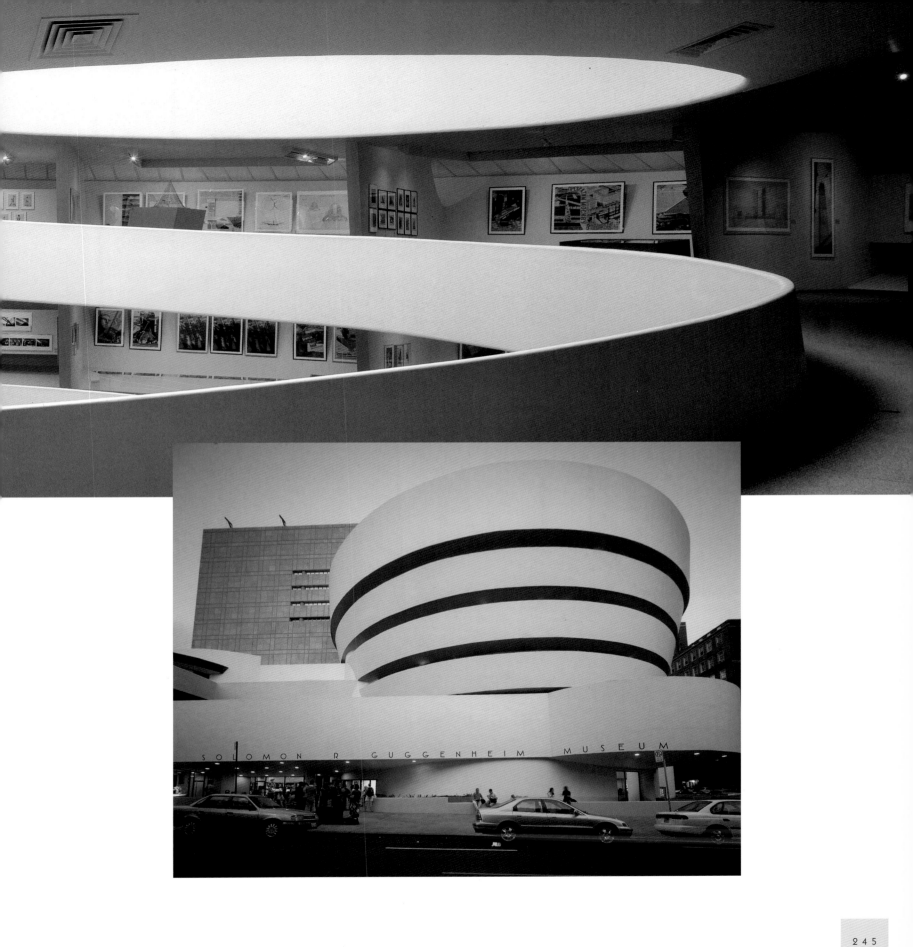

ANNUNCIATION GREEK ORTHODOX CHURCH

In a church for the Greek community in this Milwaukee suburb, a Greek cross of concrete supports a circle, one of the geometric mainstays of Wright's late career. A low dome of Middle East blue hovers over a spherical sanctuary infused with golden hues from the ceiling down to the altar screen of gold-anodized aluminum. Stained glass eyebrow windows peer over the balcony, whose circular projections and spiraling stairs echo the church's overall form. Classrooms and a dining hall are carved out below ground. Innovative yet hinting at tradition, it proved that church architecture need not be "starched stiff as a hard collar."

1956 | WAUWATOSA, WISCONSIN

MARIN COUNTY CIVIC CENTER

Progressive Marin County across the Golden Gate from San Francisco decided to break out of the governmental box by asking Wright to design a civic center for a new age. Included is his only federal commission: a post office. Concrete wings reach into the land to house administrative and judicial functions. Atriums in each bring the outdoors in; the Hall of Justice's transparent ceiling frames a view of the louvered tower. Rising by the dome at the complex's heart, it calls up the hope and unity symbolized by the Trylon and Perisphere at the 1939 World's Fair. Building of the hill, not on it, Wright ended as he began.

1957 | SAN RAPHAEL, CALIFORNIA

CHRONOLOGY

1867 Frank Lincoln (later Lloyd) Wright is born June 8 in Richland Center, Wisconsin, to Anna (Lloyd Jones) and William Cary Wright

1886 Wright briefly studies civil engineering at the University of Wisconsin

1887 Wright moves to Chicago and begins work for Joseph Lyman Silsbee

1888 Louis Sullivan's firm, Adler and Sullivan, employs Wright as a draftsman

1889 Catherine Lee Tobin and Wright marry; he designs a home for them in suburban Oak Park

1890 Frank Lloyd Wright Jr. (known as Lloyd), the first of Catherine and Frank's six children, is born; both Lloyd and his son Eric become architects

1892 Wright is the lead designer for the Charnley House in Chicago

1893 Adler and Sullivan dismisses Wright after he is found moonlighting on private commissions; he opens an office in Chicago and designs the Winslow House in River Forest

1895 Wright expands his Oak Park house, adding a dining room on the first floor and a barrel-vaulted children's playroom on the second floor

1896 "Architect, Architecture, and the Client" sets out Wright's residential ideas

1897 *House Beautiful* magazine becomes the first popular national magazine to feature Wright's work

1898 The architect builds a studio attached to his home

1901 Wright's plan for "A Home in a Prairie Town" is published in the *Ladies' Home Journal* and launches the Prairie style

1902 The Art Institute of Chicago presents the first exhibition of Wright's work, sponsored by the Chicago Architectural Club

1908 Wright designs his seminal Robie House in Chicago

1909 After creating some 120 Prairie houses, Wright leaves his family and lives in Europe with Mamah Borthwick Cheney, a client

1910 The German publisher Wasmuth publishes the first of two editions showcasing Wright's work, promoting his reputation abroad

1911 After returning the previous year, Wright builds a new home, Taliesin, in Spring Green, Wisconsin

1913 Wright obtains commissions to design Midway Gardens in Chicago and the Imperial Hotel in Tokyo, both of which are later demolished

1914 A fire destroys most of Taliesin after Mamah Cheney and six others are murdered inside by a deranged household employee

1923 Wright designs four exotic and innovative houses in the Los Angeles area; he marries Miriam Noel after Catherine divorces him

1924 Frank and Miriam separate, eventually divorcing in 1927

1925 Wright meets Olgivanna Hinzenberg, a young devotee of the mystic Gurdijieff, and she and her daughter move to Taliesin; the couple have a daughter, Iovanna, Wright's seventh child

1927 Wright first visits Arizona to consult on the Biltmore Hotel in Phoenix, returning the next year to design a resort, the never-built San Marcos-in-the-Desert

1928 Frank and Olgivanna marry

1932 Wright's *Autobiography* is published; he establishes the Taliesin Fellowship to train young architects

1936 Wright designs the first building for the maker of Johnson Wax as well as his first Usonian house, the Jacobs House, in Madison, Wisconsin

1937 Fallingwater is completed and lands Wright on the cover of *Time* magazine, refreshing his career with new public acclaim; he starts work on Taliesin West, his winter home in Scottsdale, Arizona

1938 The Taliesin Fellowship begins its annual winter migrations from Taliesin to Arizona, returning to Wisconsin in the spring

1943 Plans for the Guggenheim Museum get under way but take sixteen years; a revised *Autobiography* is published

1950 Wright designs a house for his son David and follows it three years later with one for his son Llewellyn (Robert)

1951 A retrospective exhibition, *Frank Lloyd Wright: Sixty Years of Living Architecture*, travels around the world after opening in Philadelphia, returning to New York in 1953

1954 *The Natural House* sums up Wright's principles of organic architecture

1957 The Marin County Civic Center is designed but not completed until 1962

1959 Wright continues designing into his ninety-second year, dying in Phoenix on April 9, 1959. He is buried at Unity Chapel in Spring Green, Wisconsin, the first building he worked on

FURTHER READING

Alofsin, Anthony. *Frank Lloyd Wright: The Lost Years, 1910–1922*. Chicago: University of Chicago Press, 1993.

Brooks, H. Allen. *The Prairie School: Frank Lloyd Wright and His Midwest Contemporaries*. Toronto: University of Toronto Press, 1972.

Hanks, David. *The Decorative Designs of Frank Lloyd Wright*. 1979. Reprint, New York: Dover, 1999.

Hoffmann, Donald. *Understanding Frank Lloyd Wright's Architecture*. New York: Dover, 1995.

Legler, Dixie. *Frank Lloyd Wright: The Western Work*. San Francisco: Chronicle, 1999.

———. *Prairie Style: Houses and Gardens by Frank Lloyd Wright and the Prairie School*. New York: Stewart, Tabori and Chang, 1999.

Levine, Neil. *The Architecture of Frank Lloyd Wright*. Princeton: Princeton University Press, 1996.

Lind, Carla. *Lost Wright: Frank Lloyd Wright's Vanished Masterpieces*. New York: Simon and Schuster, 1996.

———. *The Wright Style*. New York: Simon and Schuster, 1992.

Maddex, Diane. *50 Favorite Rooms/Furnishings/Houses by Frank Lloyd Wright*. 3 vols. New York: Harry N. Abrams, 1999–2000.

———. *Frank Lloyd Wright's House Beautiful*. New York: Hearst Books, 2000.

Manson, Grant Carpenter. *Frank Lloyd Wright to 1910: The First Golden Age*. New York: Van Nostrand Reinhold, 1958.

McCarter, Robert. *Frank Lloyd Wright*. London: Phaidon, 1997.

Pfeiffer, Bruce Brooks. *Frank Lloyd Wright: The Masterworks*. New York: Rizzoli, 1993.

Riley, Terence, ed., with Peter Reed. *Frank Lloyd Wright: Architect*. New York: Museum of Modern Art, 1994.

Secrest, Meryle. *Frank Lloyd Wright*. New York: Alfred A. Knopf, 1992.

Sergeant, John. *Frank Lloyd Wright's Usonian Houses: The Case for Organic Architecture*. 1976. Reprint, New York: Watson-Guptill, 1984.

Storer, William Allin. *The Frank Lloyd Wright Companion*. Chicago: University of Chicago Press, 1993.

Wright, Frank Lloyd. *Frank Lloyd Wright: Collected Writings*. 5 vols. Edited by Bruce Brooks Pfeiffer. New York: Rizzoli, 1992–95.

PHOTOGRAPH CREDITS

INDEX

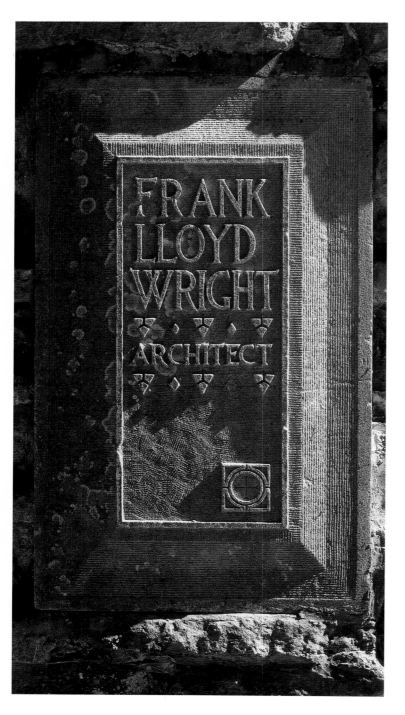

Project Director: Diane Maddex
Designer: Robert L. Wiser
Editorial Assistants: Carol Peters and Gretchen Smith Mui

The text of this book was typeset in Kabel, designed by Rudolph Koch, 1926–29.

2006 Barnes & Noble Publishing

ISBN-13: 978-0-7607-2603-7
ISBN-10: 0-7607-2603-5

Printed and bound in South Korea

5   7   9   10   8   6   4

Endpapers and chapter openers: Pyrex glass tubing in the S. C. Johnson Administration Building (1936), Racine, Wisconsin

Page 1: Wright's signature tile, Hanna House (1936), Stanford, California

Pages 2–3: Taliesin (1911), Spring Green, Wisconsin

Pages 4–5: Dana House (1902), Springfield, Illinois

Pages 6–7: Irving House (1909), Decatur, Illinois

Pages 8–9: Fallingwater (1935), Mill Run, Pennsylvania

Pages 10–11: Taliesin West (1937), Scottsdale, Arizona

Page 12: Harold Price Sr. House (1954), Paradise Valley, Arizona

Page 256: The architect's plaque, Taliesin (1911), Spring Green, Wisconsin